Meet a Baby White-Tailed Deer

Tamika M. Murray

Lerner Publications • Minneapolis

For Mom, who comforted me as we watched *Bambi*

Lerner Publications Company
An imprint of Lerner Publishing Group, Inc.
241 First Avenue North
Minneapolis, MN 55401 USA

For reading levels and more information, look up this title at www.lernerbooks.com.

Main body text set in Billy Infant Regular. Typeface provided by SparkType.

Map illustration on page 20 by Laura K. Westlund.

Library of Congress Cataloging-in-Publication Data

Names: Murray, Tamika M., author.
Title: Meet a baby white-tailed deer / Tamika M. Murray.
Description: Minneapolis : Lerner Publications, [2024] | Series: Lightning bolt books. Baby North American animals | Includes bibliographical references and index. | Audience: Ages 6–9 | Audience: Grades 2–3 | Summary: "Learn about the white-tailed deer through adorable photos and engaging text. Discover the white-tailed deer's life cycle, how it interacts with other deer, what it eats, and much more"— Provided by publisher.
Identifiers: LCCN 2022037607 (print) | LCCN 2022037608 (ebook) | ISBN 9781728491073 (lib. bdg.) | ISBN 9781728498508 (eb pdf)
Subjects: LCSH: White-tailed deer—Infancy—North America—Juvenile literature.
Classification: LCC QL737.U55 M8684 2024 (print) | LCC QL737.U55 (ebook) | DDC 599.65/21392—dc23/eng/20220809

LC record available at https://lccn.loc.gov/2022037607
LC ebook record available at https://lccn.loc.gov/2022037608

Manufactured in the United States of America
1-53038-51056-10/14/2022

Table of Contents

Birth

In the spring or summer, a baby white-tailed deer is born. It grew inside its mom for about two hundred days.

A baby white-tailed deer, a fawn, has white spots on its back and a white tail at birth. Each fawn weighs 5 to 8 pounds (2.3 to 3.6 kg). That's about the size of a newborn human baby.

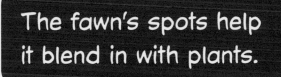

The fawn's spots help it blend in with plants.

A white-tailed deer cleans scents off her baby.

A fawn's mom licks it clean. Then predators such as bears or coyotes can't smell it.

A few hours after being born, fawns can walk. Their mom leads them to a different area to protect them from predators.

A female deer can have one to three fawns at a time.

Fawn and Mom

The mom protects her fawns. She hides her fawns so she can forage for food.

A fawn hides from predators.

The newborn fawn lays flat on the ground. It tries to blend in with the forest. It stays hidden until it hears its mom's call.

Fawns grow fast. They weigh 10 to 16 pounds (5 to 7 kg) at two weeks old. They will be 15 to 24 pounds (7 to 11 kg) when they are a month old.

A fawn stands beside its full-sized mother.

Does live in herds with their fawn or fawns.

A month-old fawn begins to follow its mom wherever she goes. The mom and fawn join a group of adult female deer, or does.

Foraging for Food

Fawns nurse from their mom several times a day. A month-old fawn forages with its mom too. The fawn stops nursing and is weaned when it is about 12 to 16 weeks old.

This fawn lives near a farm.

Just before dawn, the fawn and its mom search their habitat for food. White-tailed deer can live anywhere they can find food and hiding places. They might live in forests or near farms and swamps.

In the late afternoon, the fawn and its mom go foraging again. They eat plants including flowers, leaves, and shrubs. White-tailed deer nap when they are not foraging.

A fawn looking for food

They also need water. They will drink water from a lake, pond, puddle, or stream.

Growing Up

The fawn stays with its mom while it grows. It won't leave her side until it's at least one year old.

Adult male deer are bucks. They will join a herd of other bucks. Does can join their mother's herd or a different one.

Bucks often live in herds with two to four other males.

A buck and doe during mating season

Does can have babies when they are one or two years old. Bucks and does come together during mating season.

White-tailed deer in the wild may not reach adulthood. But when they have babies, the life cycle goes on!

White-Tailed Deer Life Cycle

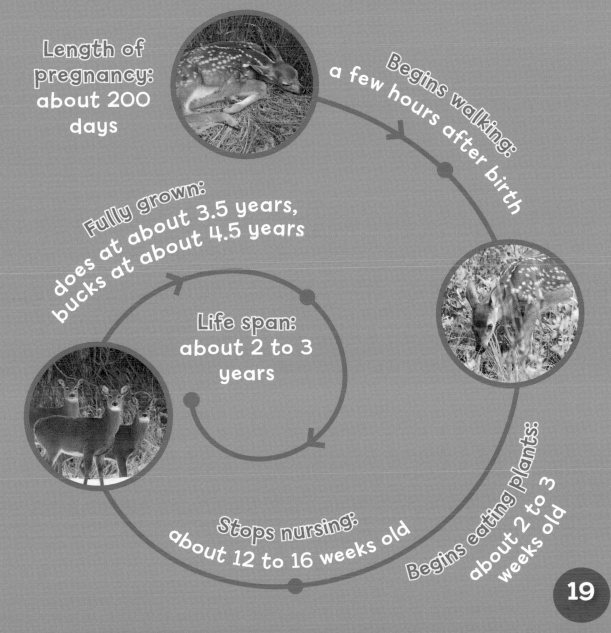

Length of pregnancy: about 200 days

Begins walking: a few hours after birth

Fully grown: does at about 3.5 years, bucks at about 4.5 years

Life span: about 2 to 3 years

Stops nursing: about 12 to 16 weeks old

Begins eating plants: about 2 to 3 weeks old

Habitat in Focus

- White-tailed deer often live on the edge of a forest by farms and brush.

- Some white-tailed deer live in thorn brush deserts in Texas and Mexico.

- Male and female white-tailed deer have separate herds.

ARCTIC OCEAN

Alaska
(US)

CANADA

Hudson
Bay

UNITED STATES

PACIFIC OCEAN

ATLANTIC OCEAN

MEXICO

Gulf of
Mexico

White-tailed
deer habitat

Country border

State/province
border

Fun Facts

- White-tailed deer can live about fifteen to twenty years in captivity.

- White-tailed deer use scent glands in their hooves to communicate with other deer.

- Most white-tailed deer lose their spots when they are three to four months old.

- White-tailed deer can run up to about 30 miles (48 km) per hour.

Glossary

doe: an adult female deer

forage: to look for food

habitat: the place where an animal lives

mating: the season when animals have babies

nurse: when an animal drinks its mother's milk

predator: an animal that kills other animals for food

wean: when an animal stops drinking its mother's milk

Learn More

Albertson, Al. *White-tailed Deer*. Minneapolis: Bellwether Media, 2020.

Bio Kids: White-Tailed Deer
http://www.biokids.umich.edu/critters/Odocoileus_virginianus/

Britannica Kids: Deer
https://kids.britannica.com/kids/article/deer/353044

PBS Nature Works: White-Tailed Deer
https://nhpbs.org/natureworks/whitetaileddeer.htm

Sabelko, Rebecca. *Baby Deer*. Minneapolis: Bellwether Media, 2022.

Schwartz, Heather E. *Meet a Baby Beaver*. Minneapolis: Lerner Publications, 2024.

Index

Photo Acknowledgments

Image credits: John Cancalosi/Alamy Stock Photo, p. 4; KenCanning/Getty Images, p. 5; Judy Freilicher/Alamy Stock Photo, p. 6; Tony Campbell/Shutterstock, p. 7; Tom Brakefield/Getty Images, p. 8; db_beyer/Getty Images, p. 9; Sankarshan Sen/500px/Getty Images, p. 10; Larry Keller, Lititz Pa./Getty Images, p. 11; arlutz73/Getty Images, p. 12; Robert Godlove/Getty Images, p. 13; Arthur Gurmankin/UIG/Getty Images, pp. 14, 19; Michel VIARD/Getty Images, p. 15; Jim Cumming/Getty Images, p. 16; KeithSzafranski/Getty Images, p. 17; Vicki Jauron, Babylon and Beyond Photography/Getty Images, p. 18.

Cover credit: Betty Shelton/Shutterstock.